YO GOD!

Can You Hook Me Up With a Wave!?

YO
GOD!

*Can You Hook Me
Up With a Wave!?*

ROB ROBINSON

Carpenter's Son Publishing

Yo God! Can You Hook Me Up with a Wave?!

©2016 by Rob Robinson

Published by Carpenter's Son Publishing, Franklin, Tennessee.

Published in association with Larry Carpenter of Christian Book Services, LLC. www.christianbookservices.com

Scripture quotations marked (TLB) are taken from The Living Bible copyright © 1971. Used by permission of Tyndale House Publishers, Inc., Carol Stream, Illinois 60188. All rights reserved.

Edited by Shirelle Roberts

Cover and Interior Layout Design by Suzanne Lawing

Printed in the United States of America

978-1-942587-97-2

The LORD on high is mightier than the noise of
many waters, yea, than the mighty waves of the sea

—Psalm 93:4

DEDICATION

Special thanks to Brother Danny. I only met you once and I don't know your last name, but your testimony impacted my life and will impact the lives of all who read this book.

Thank you, Sister Maratha Wheeler, blessing from the Most High, for your obedience in being a witness for Him and for leading Danny to his new life in Christ.

The sea hath no king but God alone . . .

—Dante Gabriel Rossetti

CONTENTS

FOREWORD

In the week of July 4th 2017, my husband and I went to the Jersey Shore for vacation. The trip had been planned for months. I never envisioned how much I'd begin to love the ocean and its beaches during that time in my life. I've always had a great respect for the sea, but also a great fear of its possibilities as it relates to swimmers of all kinds. I'd heard many tragic stories of how many lives the ocean had claimed throughout my lifetime. The numbers never cease. Regrettably, sometimes even the most experienced swimmers lose their lives battling unforgivable currents and riptides. It is true, the sea shall someday give up its dead (Rev 20:13): however, that didn't stop me from enjoying the cool of the waves as they rolled over my feet at the shoreline.

At one point, I became very brave and decided to walk out a little further, than I had previously done during that week. Somehow, I slipped and fell backwards. The waves began coming like labor pains every 60 seconds before I could catch my breath. I was only four feet from the shoreline, four feet! The current threw me around like sand granules on the bottom of the ocean. In those seconds of what seemed to be a lifetime, panic set in and I forgot that I could swim. Many people watched from the shoreline as I tried frantically, to get my feet on solid ground. All I could hear were the children screaming and yelling, "Miss, are you alright, are you ok?" Little did they know that I was drowning.

By the grace of God, I managed to finally turn over and stand to my feet as the waves pushed me to the shoreline. At the time of this fiasco, I was reading the draft of this book, *"Yo God! Can You Hook Me Up With a Wave?!"* Ironically, I thought that the Lord was being very facetious, intending to teach me some hidden lesson.

Days later I considered what I thought was the purpose of that frightful day. Maybe I needed to be a partaker of what it felt like to be rescued by an all-seeing God in a turbulent situation, like the character of this book. I needed to feel what he felt, during those frightful minutes of his life in which nobody but God could hear his cries for help. You may ask, "But why would God do that to you?"

Previously, I told Rob that I did not have the time to help with this books production. A couple of days later however, I called to share what happened during our vacation. I believed the Lord wanted me not only to make time to help with the project, but also to glean from the divine process of supplication this family took, to get unconventional miracles through prayer.

"Yo God! Can You Hook Me Up With a Wave?!" is full of miracles, expectations, encouragement, and divine direction on how to get a miracle from The Lord, even when it looks impossible. Read the true stories in this book and let them elevate your walk with God by giving you a *"Crazy"* kind of Faith. Thank

you, Rob Robinson. You've written another beautiful manuscript that helped to raise another level of my faith, this time in the Power of God through prayer, which I did not have previously!

—SHIRELLE ROBERTS
CEO of Fountain of Living Water Publishing
Former Assistant Manager of CLC Book
Center

PREFACE

The book *"Yo God! Can You Hook Me Up With a Wave?!"*, was birthed out of a cry of desperation from a young man of his miraculous rescue from drowning. Without knowing it, his testimony which was shared at an evening worship service, gave hope and inspiration to those who were in attendance. Many of us at the time, were treading in the tidal waves of life. The young man's testimony helped to build my faith. It further motivated me to write this book, in an effort to build your faith in God, as well as elevate the faith of others.

Isn't it surprising, that from the least likely of places we can find encouragement? If life seems overwhelming, hang on to hope. Even if you find yourself overloaded with bills, a medical condition, or a major hurdle in your life that seems impossible, never give up. Do not throw in the towel, because there is help for you down the road. You may not be able to see it now, but like a wave it's coming.

Through the examples and testimonies in this book, you will find that with the help of the Most High, there is no problem in life that is so insurmountable, that with God you cannot solve: nothing so impossible that He cannot change and nothing unbeatable that Christ alone has not conquered. Be encouraged, *"God is our refuge and strength, a very present help in trouble"* (Psalm 46:1).

ACKNOWLEDGMENTS

Special thanks go out to the following people for contributions in helping to bring this project to fruition. Your assistance is greatly appreciated. May the Most High bless you and keep you.

Shirelle Roberts
Mary Maduzia
Hang Ho
Charlie Hu

INTRODUCTION

Like a roaring sea, the waves of life can either kill us or push us through turbulent waters of affliction. Grabbing ahold of faith feels out of reach, when what you see with your naked eye looks impossible. The adversity, when we are in the midst of it, somehow feels bigger than our God! We often cry out "Lord where are you in all of this? Have you forgotten about me? Help Father I'm dying!" The more we maneuver to get out of the circumstances we're in, the deeper we are pulled under a sea of disaster.

The young man in this book found himself in a dangerous position, because of his lack of obedience to the rules that were posted; like some of us who have found ourselves in life threatening situations, because of our own doing. As believers, trouble can sometimes knock on our doors when we fail to appropriate written instructions in God's Word. Trials either build our faith, while teaching us to trust in God, or, chasten our inability to submit to the potter's wheel of spiritual growth. Without a doubt, God orchestrates the trials of life and He certainly knows what He wants to accomplish in and through us. If He orchestrates our trials, then it will take God to get us out of them. (Job 42:10). *"Yo God! Can You Hook Me Up With a Wave?!"*

It's up to God to do the judging. You haven't walked in my boots, so how are you going to judge me?

—Aaron Neville

CHAPTER ONE

CHURCH PROFILING

According to Merriam Webster's Dictionary, profiling is described as *"the act or practice of regarding particular people as more likely to commit crimes because of their appearance, race, etc."* Let me submit to you, that without a doubt, the church has long exercised such behavior for centuries. In fact, church profiling is alive and well among denominations across America still today. Regrettably, I stand to be counted in that number. It was a Wednesday night in the summer of 1996. My family and I attended a ministry that was a church plant from Detroit, Michigan. The church met in the former Holiday Inn on City Line Avenue in Philadelphia, Pennsylvania.

That particular Wednesday night, the prayer service started out a little differently from previous services. The pastor began the service by giving members and guests an opportunity for testimony. Looking back, this is the only time in my ten-year membership, that

I can recall an old-fashioned testimony service being held before a Wednesday night midweek service.

Members got up and testified of the goodness of the Lord. They praised Him for healing, deliverance and providing for their families. It was a blessed and enjoyable time.

Finally, because of the lateness of the hour, the pastor announced that we had time for one more testimony. It was then that a young man sitting in the seat in front of me spoke up and said, "Pastor, I want to say something." The pastor responded, "Go ahead, brother."

This young man, who did not resemble any of us, stood and gave one of the most anointed, sincere, and heartfelt testimonies that I have ever heard. But I am getting ahead of my story.

In the middle of the testimony service, Sister Maratha Wheeler, a member of the church, walked down the middle aisle accompanied by a young man named Danny. I would describe Danny as a person who looked like a member of a motorcycle gang who'd just gotten off his Harley Davidson motorcycle. I would dare to say his harsh appearance seemed to be evident of his life. It looked as if all the partying, drinking, and drug use, had aged him beyond his years. He had long, stringy, uncombed hair, along with tattoos covering every inch of his arms. He wore dingy jeans that were frayed at the bottom from dragging the ground. The bottoms of his pant legs were cut out in the back in the shape of a upside down U from constant wear. It looked as if his jeans were designed that way, because the heels of his boots peaked back at you through the upside down U shape of his hemline.

There was a silver chain connected to a pant loop on the right side of his jeans. The other end was connected to a brown leather billfold in his right back pocket. One-quarter of the billfold stuck out of the top of the pocket, and the tip of it peeked out through a hole in the bottom of the pocket.

Danny wore a black t-shirt with some kind of punk rock design on the front. His boots were brown, worn, and run over; they reminded me of a pair of old cowboy boots you'd see on an old western movie. His ears were pierced. However, I'm not sure how many earrings he was wearing, I could see at least two in each ear and his hair obstructed my ability to see any additional piercings. In addition, he wore black leather wristbands tightly wrapped around each arm, along with other bangles, bracelets, and wristlets.

In other words, he was dressed exactly opposite of the typical church member you'd see every Sunday morning at an 11:00 a.m. service.

I, with my sanctified holier-than-thou dignified self, immediately placed him at the Great White Throne Judgment. In fact, I judged Danny as soon as I saw him walk down the aisle to take his seat. I murmured in my heart, asking what this young man could possibly say that would glorify our Awesome Creator. I mean look how he was dressed! Sardonically, I thought to myself, *He's going to testify for God looking like a Hell's Angel?*

Being a Bible college graduate, missionary, praise

and worship leader, pastor, preacher, and Bible teacher, I should have known better. Matthew 7:1–2 reads, *"Judge not, that ye be not judged. For with what judgment ye judge, ye shall be judged: and with what measure ye mete, it shall be measured to you again."* In Luke 6:37, we are advised, *"Judge not, and you shall not be judged: condemn not, and ye shall not be condemned: forgive, and ye will be forgiven."*

Verse 9 of the parable reads, *"And He spake this parable unto certain which trusted in themselves that they were righteous, and despised others."*

This verse tells us that some religious people trust in their own righteousness while despising the righteousness of others. I acted similar to the Pharisee in the story and exalted myself above Danny, while at the same time despising him. I looked at his appearance and his mannerisms and said to myself, "What can he tell me? What could he possibly say that would be relevant to the service?"

Verse 10 reads, *"Two men went up to the temple to pray, one a Pharisee and the other a publican."*

Although sometimes you will see the term "tax collector" in place of publican, the Bible was not talking about Republicans here—a publican is another name for a tax collector. I believe that the verse describes an actual event of two men going to the temple to pray. In like manner on that Wednesday night in 1996, I went to a prayer meeting to pray, and so did Danny go to the same prayer meeting to pray. However, instead of praying for Danny, our visitor, I judged and ridiculed him. I did not even know him, and I passed judgment.

How many of us judge people by what we see, or by what we've heard others say about them? How many of us measure others by our own standards? Danny was there to pray and to give the Most High glory and praise. Unbeknownst to me, he was about to share a testimony that would strongly influence my life.

Verse 11 of Luke 18 states, *"The Pharisee stood and prayed thus with himself, 'God, I thank Thee, that I am not like other men are, extortioners, unjust, adulterers, or even as this publican.'"* The Pharisee prayed a selfish prayer full of pride, arrogance, and judgment against other men, particularly the tax collector.

There is no room in the kingdom of God for behavior such as that exhibited by the Pharisee or even me on that particular evening. A religion based upon a merit system leads to religious pride, two verses of Scripture brings this to light. Proverbs 16:5 says, *"Everyone that is proud in heart is an abomination to the LORD; though hand join in hand, he shall not be unpunished."* Likewise, in Proverbs 16:18, we learn, *"Pride goeth before destruction, and a haughty spirit before a fall."* I realized that I sat in the midweek service with the same pharisaical spirit towards Danny as the Pharisee exhibited towards the tax collector in the parable.

Jesus said, *"I tell you, this man went down to his house justified rather than the other; for everyone who exalteth himself will be abased; and he that humbleth himself will be exalted."* Indeed, in 1 John 1:9 we read, *"If we confess our sins, He is faithful and just to forgive us our sins, and to cleanse us from all unrighteousness."*

These two verses work in conjunction with each other to teach us the value of humility; the importance of recognizing our sins, and the necessity of confession. Only there can we find true forgiveness.

As you read on, you will see how the words of the entire parable of the Pharisee and the publican are pure truth. Who are we to say who is or is not a child of God based upon a person's appearance? Who are we to say whose heart is pure? We are not, or should I say, I am not in any position to pass judgment. In so instructing, Psalm 44:21 asks, *"Shall not God search this out? For He knoweth the secrets of the heart."*

We do not know where, or how much, or from what the Father has delivered others. We are not equipped to judge, nor to offer grace, it belongs to God alone. (James 4:6)

For a moment, my self-righteous attitude caused me to forget my own flaws. If Danny and I had gone home to be with the LORD, he would have stood in the presence of God purely more justified than I.

Prayer begins where human capacity ends.

—MARIAN ANDERSON

CHAPTER TWO

YO GOD! CAN YOU HOOK ME UP WITH A WAVE?!

Getting back to Danny's testimony. After thanking the pastor for granting him the opportunity to speak, he explained that he was newly saved and needed a change in his life. Sister Martha had witnessed to him about embarking on a new life in Christ and led him in the prayer of repentance a couple of weeks prior to our service. Danny testified that drugs, alcohol, and sex had filled his life, but ceased in bringing him the peace and satisfaction he so desired. So, he made the choice to receive Christ as his Lord and Savior and became a born-again believer in *Christ*.

On this night however, he came to church to tell us of a life altering event that changed his life. If you will allow me to re-enact the testimony, about a week before, he had gone swimming at the New Jersey shore. Danny made an awful decision to go for a swim alone. This area had no lifeguards and very few people walking the beach. It was a blistering, hot, sweltering day and all he could think about was the relief of the refreshing ocean waters so, in he went. He was enjoying his time in the ocean so much so, that he did not realize the undertow had gradually pulled him farther and farther away from the shoreline. As he faced the open waters, he then decided to turn and look back at the shore. He was shocked beyond belief how far offshore he had drifted.

The thought crossed his mind that this may not have been such a good idea after all. He was so far offshore that no one could hear him as he yelled for help. No one even noticed him.

As he started his way toward the shoreline, he found himself caught in a rip current.

He'd swim for a few feet, and then the rip current would pull him back out. He tried to swim a few more feet, but the rip current continued to pull him out again. This cycle repeated itself over and over again.

He became so exhausted from trying to stay above water. It felt as if he'd been doing this for hours. He then remembered Sister Maratha telling him that "God is just a prayer away." He thought to himself that he should pray and ask God for help. Not knowing how to pray he looked up towards the sky and cried out with a loud voice, *"Yo God! Can You Hook Me Up With A Wave?!"*

You could hear the proverbial pin drop as a hush came over the congregation. Everyone listened intensively to hear the outcome of this young man's testimony.

Danny acted out his story, showing the group how he came up for air, explaining that, at the time, he felt each gasp could possibly be his last. He demonstrated how he turned around to see if the Father had answered his cry for help. He showed how he wiped the seawater from his eyes so that he could see.

When he opened his eyes, there was a massive wave heading right for him. He had just enough time to turn, face the shore, place his arms over his head, and hold his hands together as if he were diving. With seconds to go, he took a deep breath to ride the wave as it pushed him forward.

The wave covered him and bounced him side to side and up and down like a rubber ball. As he felt himself slow down, he eventually came to a complete stop. He popped his head up out of the water as he tried to catch his breath. The wave was no longer strong enough to carry him as it continued to its destination.

Again, Danny was left treading water, still too tired and too far away to swim to shore. However, defeat had been cast out of his thoughts, and hope swelled within his heart because the Father had heard and answered his prayer. He was now closer to the shore, and his faith began to rise.

After a minute or two, the weariness again crawled through his legs and arms. The rip current was pulling him back out to sea while gravity was pulling him down once more.

He went underneath the water for a brief time to rest his muscles. He mustered up the strength to forge his way back to the surface. After wiping the saltwater from his face, Danny looked, and there, unbelievably, was a second wave, as immense as the first, heading in his direction. There was scarcely time for him to turn, face the shore, and place his arms and hands above his head as he had done previously.

Danny took a deep breath just as the wave hit him, thrusting him forward. The energy of the wave gradually died down, causing it to lose its momentum. Though the wave continued, it did not have the strength to move him any closer to the shore. The wave did move him; however, it fell short of helping him achieve his ultimate goal of reaching the golden sands of the shore line.

He was in an all-too-familiar position, treading water and trying to keep his head above water so that he could remain alive. He knew that the ocean floor had a gradual slope and, thought that maybe he was close enough to reach it.

He stretched out his right leg as far as he could, swishing it around and hoping to feel granules of sand on the ocean floor with his toes. He first tried his right leg, then the left leg, then his right leg, then his left again, always maintaining his head above the water. Underwater, it must have looked like he was on a Stairmaster® exercise machine as he went back and forth with each leg. He soon realized it was futile to waste precious energy; he was still too far away from the shoreline.

Danny was so close and yet so far away. Fear gripped him. Thoughts of *you'll never make it, you're going to die, there's no use,* and *you might as well give up,* raced through his mind. But through the doubt and negative voices bombarding his thoughts, one voice shone forth—the voice of Sister Maratha. She had encouraged Danny with enough of the Word on that day that it carried him through this entire ordeal. Danny looked back to where he had started treading water and struggling to get to shore. He turned and looked at the shoreline, calculating the distance he had to go to reach safety. He knew that it was the The Most High who had brought him this far. He knew that it would have to be the Father who would bring him all the way home. But should he dare ask for another wave? Would he be bugging the Father? Would the Father even listen?

Danny looked up to the sky and spoke to the Father. He said, "So God, I'm trusting and I'm praying for Your help one more time . . . well, God . . I don't know any other way to say it but . . ." He sighed and cried out, "*Yo God! Can You Hook Me Up With a Wave?!*"

Danny looked out in the vast ocean and noticed a certain section beginning to rise. It became bigger and bigger and bigger until it formed into a huge third wave, aiming right for him like an arrow to a bullseye.

He quickly looked up and said, "Thank you, God." He turned, placed his arms and hands over his head, and let out a scream. "Yee haw!" He must have sounded like a cowboy riding a bucking bronco on a ranch. This is ironic because the wave hit him fast and furiously like a bull bursting out of a chute.

Danny was in for the ride of his life, because his life depended on it. He mounted this two-thousand-pound steer and was determined to ride it the full eight seconds or however much time he needed to reach the sandy shore.

The wave bucked, reared, kicked, spun, and twisted—not in an effort to throw its rider off but to get him to his appointed destination. It seemed to be under strict orders to get him there, and it was not deviating one iota from its assignment.

Danny was also unwavering in riding this wave until every ounce of energy was drained out of it and could not transport him any longer. He continued to hold his breath even though his lungs frantically cried out for deliverance. To breathe was a formidable foe; however, Danny took control of the urge and stayed the course.

The wave stopped bucking; kicking and twisting, but it still maintained its speed. He was no longer riding bull or breaking in a wild stallion. It was more like he was riding a thoroughbred horse racing down the home stretch, heading for the finish line at Belmont in the final race of the Triple Crown. Unbeknownst to Danny, above him the wave began to steepen, and the crest became unstable, causing turbulent white-water to spill down the face of the wave. As the wave approached the shore, the wave's momentum slowly dissipated in the whitewater, spilling over and over until it created a relatively gentle wave so calm that it finally came to an end.

Having come to a complete stop and still not on the shore, Danny raised his head out of the water and inhaled the biggest quantity of air he had ever taken in his life. He breathed so uncontrollably until he was able to catch his breath. His energy was far spent, but he knew the ordeal was far from over.

It was then he felt something brush against the big toe of his right foot. He stretched out his right leg, and there it was again. It felt like granules. He stretched his left leg, feeling around with his toes, and he found the grainy substance with that leg as well. It was particles of sand flowing between his toes!

After the most tumultuous time of his life, He was finally touching the ocean floor with his toes. The water was still too deep for him to place his whole foot on the ocean floor.

He was too exhausted to swim, so using a breast-stroke technique and walking, he gradually moved toward the level ocean floor. Coordinating his breast-stroke with each step, he sluggishly moved at a snail's pace digging his toes deeper and deeper into the sandy ocean floor. Strokes by stroke and step by step, more of his feet were touching the ocean floor. Finally, he was standing flat-footed. The water level was just below his chin.

He paused to rest for a moment.

Frighteningly, Danny felt the tug of the under-tow fighting to pull him out to the watery abyss. The undertow was not as strong as the rip current, but it still relentlessly tried to pull him back out to the depths of the sea. However, the ocean underestimated his inexorable will to live, especially now that he had seen the Most High move three times on his behalf by sending three waves to rescue him. There was no way he was going to be sucked back out to sea.

Gathering himself, without thinking, he began to run. He forgot all about swimming and just started running, reminiscent of Tom Hanks in the movie *Forrest Gump*. All Danny could think was, "Run, Danny. *Run!*"

As he moved, the water level dropped from his chest to his stomach to his waist. It was finally over. He slowed his pace to a walk and trudged out of the ocean like a groom down the aisle at a shotgun wedding.

As he raised his hands, they looked like prunes, wet and wrinkly. Danny lumbered straight ahead on dry sand, closed his eyes, spun around and collapsed on his back.

With his eyes shut, he listened attentively with a new-found respect for the cawing of the seagulls and the splashing waves of the Jersey Shore. They were music to his ears. He had survived a life-and death situation and lived to tell it. At that moment, he propped himself up and rested on his elbows. He took a long gaze at the massive ocean and breathed a big sigh of relief.

Sluggishly, he stood up. His entire hind parts were covered in sand, but at this point, he really didn't care. He turned and walked to his car. Miraculously, he was homeward bound. Danny walked approximately ten feet and realized that he forgot to do something. He stopped, smiled, glanced back at the ocean, looked up toward the sky, and yelled, "Yo God! Thanks for hooking me up with a wave?!"

As he concluded his story, the anointing of the Holy Spirit filled the room. The *Wa Ruwach* (The Holy Spirit) was clearly present in the room, and a *Tahillah* praise (spontaneous praise) erupted.

Church members, including me, leapt to their feet and lifted their voices to praise the Most High. Some sat and raised their hands in praise. Others clapped their hands and cried out, "Glory!" "Praise the Lord!" "Bless His Holy Name!"

Sister Maratha sat next to her guest with her right arm raised, her hand waving in an offering of praise. Tears escaped from her eyes as if in a slow race, rolling past the finish line. Sister Maratha looked up toward heaven, saying over and over again, "Thank You, Jesus; Thank You, Jesus; Thank you, Jesus!"

The congregation's reaction caused Danny to survey the room with a surprised and puzzled look as if he was thinking, *what just happened?* He did not fully understand the truth and the power of his words. However, the people knew and could relate.

Members of the congregation may have never experienced what it felt like to be drowning in the ocean, but they too had experienced some form of financial or medical situations that were so overwhelming, that it seemed they too were drowning.

Many were also privy to the first two verses of Psalm 121 which reads, *"I will lift up my eyes to the hills, from whence cometh my help. My help cometh from the LORD, which made heaven and earth."*

I'm not sure if Danny knew any of those verses in the Book of Psalms to quote at that moment. Sadly, in a moment of what seemed like a twinkling of an eye, Danny was in dire straits in the ocean of New Jersey. Thinking about his situation:

- He did not have time to call his pastor.
- He did not have time to call his prayer partner.
- He did not have time to call the deacons.
- He did not have time to call the phone prayer line.
- He did not have time to wait for Wednesday night prayer meeting.

None of these options were available to him at the time. Therefore, Danny did the only thing he could do and that was to look to the hill from which supplied his help. So, with a loud voice he cried, *"Yo God! Can You Hook Me Up With a Wave?!"*

He was not in the least bit concerned with how religious he sounded. He had no time to be religiously correct saying things like, "Thou Holiest and most gracious Father heareth now as thy servant prayeth to thee . . ." His prayer was short, unorthodox and straight to the point.

It was more street than church. However, the most important thing was that it was a sincere, heartfelt prayer.

- When you are drowning and desperately seeking help from the Lord, you don't care who's around, who hears you, or how you appear to others. You need a wave of divine intervention and you need it *NOW!!*

- When you are drowning in a sea of debt, you need to cry out with a prayer of desperation like Danny.

- When the doctor says, he has done all he can do, and he tells you he can't do anymore, again you need to cry out. (Psalm 34:6)

Whatever ocean you may find yourself drowning in, forget man's traditions; forget the rituals, forget the customs. You need to look to heaven and cry with a loud voice, *"Yo God! Can You Hook Me Up With a Wave?!"* (A Miracle!)

When thou passest through the waters,
I will be with thee; and through the rivers they
shall not overflow thee: when thou walkest through
the fire, thou shalt not be burned; neither shall the
flame kindle upon thee. For I am the LORD thy God,
the Holy One of Israel, thy Saviour . . .

—Isaiah 43:2, 3a

CHAPTER THREE

WHY THREE WAVES?

After Danny gave his inspiring testimony, I asked the Father, "Danny asked you for a wave, but why did you send three waves?" (I am just curious that way.)

I believe that He spoke to me and said, "I sent three waves, one for the Father, one for the Son, and one for the Holy Spirit."

Later, as I meditated on what the Father said, I received further explanation. When a born-again believer in Christ is in trouble and cries out to the Father for help, the Trinity, or God Head, Father, Son and the Holy Spirit gets involved.

In his book, *Biblical Mathematics: Keys to scripture Numerics,* evangelist Ed F. Vallowe writes that the number three came to "*carry the thought of the Divine. It means God is in it. It is the number of divine completeness and perfection.*"

1. *Christ is the Way, The Truth, The Life* (John 14:6).

2. *He raised THREE from the dead during His earthly ministry. (The Widow's son, Jairu's daughter, and Lazarus)*

3. *He was crucified at the THIRD HOUR*

4. *There was THREE hours of darkness when He was on the Cross.*

5. *He rose the THIRD DAY.*
NO other number in all the Bible reveals the works of the Creator than the number THREE.[1]

In retrospect, Danny's story reminded me of a similar situation in which I found myself in several years earlier.

In 1989, I went to Haiti on my first mission trip. It was a first for me in three respects. It was the first time I flew on an airplane. It was also the first time I left the borders of the continental United States. Finally, as mentioned, it was my first mission trip. Can you see the pattern of three representing the Divine Completeness and Perfection of these occurrences?

At the time, I was the pastor of a church in Norristown, Pennsylvania, called Church of New Life. We were part of an organization called Resurrection, Churches, and Ministries (RCM). The mission ministry of RCM was called Team World Outreach (TWO).

In the summer of 1989, two members of our church Valerie Lawson and Monica Robinson (my wife), felt they were called of God to go on a missions trip to Haiti. However, I did not feel the leading of the Lord to accompany them. I felt there was enough ministry in the United States and, we did not have to go to a foreign country to help those in need. Without question, I was willing to do all I could to help the two of them fulfill the LORDS call.

As pastor of Church of New Life, the leadership of RCM suggested that I attend the trip, feeling it would be an invaluable experience for me (seeing I'd never been on a missions trip before). They felt that my participation as a leader would set an example for Church of New Life members. At the time, workers were scarce in the vineyard. So, I had a conversation with the Father. My talk with Him was on the order of Gideon's conversation in Judges 6:36–40 when he wanted assurance that it was the Father asking him to lead the Children of Israel in battle against the Midianites. I felt, the best way to know of a surety that God was sending me to accompany the women to Haiti, was to also put out a fleece. I said, "Father, if it is your will, then you will have to provide the money for me to go. I will help raise money for Monica and Valerie, but you have to provide the money for me to go."

The church held yard sales, sent out support letters, and asked family, friends, and coworkers for donations. Secretly, I'd hoped that we would not raise enough money so that I could digress. Wouldn't you know it; we raised enough money to send all three of us. There is the number three again (Divine Completeness and Perfection).

There was a total of eleven team members on the mission trip. Half stayed in Port-au-Prince, the capital of Haiti, while I and the rest of us (We called ourselves the A-Team) went to minister in the village of Balix. We set up a temporary clinic in Balix that was two and a half to three hours from the capital. We ministered to a total of 200 - 300 hundred people in three days (Divine Completeness and Perfection) during the day and held evangelistic services at night.

Now when I say set up a clinic, please do not picture a clean, sterile building with all the necessary equipment and medicines to take care of every sickness and disease. It was far from that.

The clinic structure had a tin lean-to, also called a shed roof, held up by young trees that measured roughly ten feet high and six inches in diameter. There were no walls, windows, doors, indoor plumbing of any kind, or electricity. The furniture consisted of several rows of plank wood nailed to tree stumps. The wood was not planed but was smooth from wear. There were additional rows of plastic lawn chairs, handmade wooden chairs, and whatever people could find to sit on.

The structure held approximately one hundred people within its boundaries. The "building" was of a multipurpose use and functioned as the village church, school, meeting hall, and clinic. The floor of the structure was simply the ground. Before every church service, some of the village women sprinkled water on the ground and swept the dirt with a bale palmis (a short handheld broom instrument). They did this to keep the dust to a minimum. While they worked, the women sang songs and offered up prayers to the Most High.

I want to go down a rabbit trail if you'll permit me and tell you a brief story. You know that the Father has a sense of humor.

On our first night in the village, a church service was held in the village church, New World Missions for Christ, Pastor Carlo Thomas. It was dark. Richard Grubb, our missions' trip leader, delivered the message that night. Our translator, Robert, held a flashlight so that Richard could see his notes and read Scripture. I sat in the front of the congregation behind Richard.

Just off to his right and almost out of my peripheral vision, I kept seeing an orange object. I did not want to bring attention to myself, so I slowly turned my head to the right. Standing there was a little Haitian boy, maybe nine or ten years old, wearing an orange Philadelphia Flyers hockey team jersey. I almost burst out laughing.

Here I was in a village in Haiti, a four-and-a-half-hour plane ride from Philadelphia, and here was a little boy wearing an NHL Jersey from the Major League Hockey team from Philly. What are the odds that I would be in a church service in a village in Haiti at the same time that a Haitian boy was wearing a Philadelphia Flyers Jersey?

I took it as a humorous message from the Father that I was in His Divine Will. Remember that I did not want to go on the trip, and here was the Father letting me know that it was His will for me to be at that place, at just that time, for His purpose. But I digress.

At our clinic, Haitians came from miles around seeking help for all types of ailments, broken bones, burns, and STDs (that is another story for another time).

After the final day of the clinic, we were exhausted. We looked at each other and yelled, "Beach!" That was our ritual each day when the clinic closed. This would be our last day at the beach because the next day we were leaving to go back to Port-au-Prince. So, we all went to the beach.

The beach did not have the soft sand to which we were accustomed—in fact, it was very rocky. The women in our group, Valerie, Patricia, Kathy, and Deborah, would lay out on the sand, soaking up the sun. The villagers, young and old, male and female, came down to the beach and stood about ten feet behind us, while others sat on boats resting alongside of us. Some brought their animals, horses, cows, goats, and dogs and stood around.

I asked our translator, Robert, why the villagers were standing behind us. He said, "They are here to watch you."

"To watch us," I replied. "Why would they want to watch us?"

Suddenly, it struck me. With no electricity, there were also no phones, no television, no CD or DVD players, no radios, no Wi-Fi, no computers, no Wii, no PlayStation, no cable, and no satellite: we were the villagers' entertainment for the day. They came to see the crazy Americans lay out in the sun, try to walk barefoot on the rocky shore, run from the little lizards, and act like it was our first time at the shore. We were not as bad as the cast from the reality show Jersey Shore, but we were still entertaining in a clean way.

Valerie, Patricia, Kathy, and Deborah ventured into the water up to their knees and thighs, splashing around a little bit and then go right back to sunbathing. The water was rough, so you couldn't really blame them. Our team leader, Richard, and I were more adventurous and swam through the rough waters up to our chest until it became tranquil, deceptively so.

Richard and his family had lived in Haiti for four years. He was very knowledgeable about the culture and customs, and was fluent in Haitian Creole, which is used for most everyday communication. A minority of the population also speak French, which they have learned either at home or at school.

Richard and I were relaxing in the peaceful water talking about the day's events and life in general. The setting was so serene, we did not realize that the undertow was gradually pulling us out to sea. I told you the serenity of the water was deceptive. I said to Richard, "Wow! Look how far out those three Haitian boys are."

Note the number three—Divine Completeness and Perfection. Three Haitian boys had joined us but left us and swam farther out into the Caribbean Sea. They were so far out that their heads resembled three coconuts floating in the water.

Richard said, "That's nothing! Look how far out we are." I looked back at the shore, and the people on the shore looked like they were the size of little Lego® figurines.

I'm not going to lie, I got scared. I said to Richard, "I don't know about you, but I'm heading to shore." Richard said to go ahead, but that he was going to stay out and chill a little more.

I turned and started swimming to the shore. The swim began fairly effortlessly, but soon I found myself in the clutches of a riptide. It seemed like the harder I swam towards the shore, the harder the riptide pulled me out to sea. The struggle to reach the shore drained every ounce of energy I had. I was in a predicament similar to Danny's whereby I was caught in the grips of a riptide.

There was no more strength in my body. I was at the point of drowning . . . I thought I was going to die and my body would be washed out to sea. I was at the mercy of the sea, my heart was racing, and I started to panic.

I calmed myself down and said to the Lord, "I don't want to go like this. I don't want to die like this."

My life did not flash before my eyes, but I did picture my wife (who was with the other mission team back in Port-au-Prince), my then six-year-old daughter, my nine-year-old son, and my mother, who was back in the United States praying for us. I did not want them to have to live without me (Thanks to the Most High for a praying mother).

A Bible story came to mind where Jesus said to the disciples, *"let us pass over to the other side"* (Mark 4:35). They all got into a boat and began sailing to the other side.

"And there arose a great storm of wind, and the waves

beat into the ship, so that it was now full" (Mark 4:37). "And He was in the hinder part of the ship, asleep on a pillow and they awake him, and say unto him, Master, carest thou not that we perish"? (Mark 4:38)

That is how I was feeling in that moment, when I was afraid and caught in the riptide. *Carest thou not that I perish?*

I said, "Father I'm out in the Caribbean Sea about to drown, I need your help!"

Right then, the thought came to me to ride the waves in and swim when the water receded. *"If any of you lack wisdom, let him ask of God, that giveth to all men liberally, and upbraideth not; and it shall be given him"* (James 1:5).

So, when the next wave rolled my way, I rode it as long as it would carry me. It did not take long before I was surrounded by a wave that loaded me like a Mark 48 torpedo in a tube and expelled me as a human missile toward the shore. It felt as though I was riding in the front car of an old wooden roller coaster being tossed around like a rag doll. Riding the wave gave me time to rest a bit when it stopped, I knew that I would have to continue to swim against the riptide. The wave died down and rest time was over.

The riptide began pulling on me like a one-Tesla electromagnetic crane lifting scrap ferrous metals in a recycling plant. When your life is at stake, it is amazing what comes to your mind in order to survive.

My mind flashed back to when I learned how to swim at my hometown's YMCA. Brian, my swimming instructor, taught me to cup my hands, reach out, and push the water back with each stroke. He taught me to kick from my hips and not from my knees. I believe it was the *Wa Ruwach* (The Holy Spirit) that reminded me of this. I implemented the correct swimming technique immediately, cupping my hands, kicking from my hips, and swimming with all my might.

I have watched several nature shows telling the story of the life of a salmon. After experiencing the strength of an undertow, I have a much greater appreciation for how difficult it is for salmon swimming upstream against the current to spawn and secure the survival of the next generation. They are determined to reach their destination, and they will continue to fight until they arrive at their objective. The verse, *"I shall not die, but live, and declare the works of the LORD,"* (Psalm 118:17) came to my mind, and I became as determined as a salmon to get out of that water and see my family again.

The riptide still had me in its tractor beam (For all you Star Trek fans) until its hold was broken by a second wave. The wave hit with intense power, violently lunging me forward, as if I was rafting down whitewater rapids, but without a boat.

Even though the wave thrashed me around vigorously, I was able to get a little rest for my muscles. When the wave diminished, and the tug-of-war with the riptide commenced again, I wiped the saltwater from my face and was briefly able to look at the shoreline and see that Valerie, Patricia, Kathy, and Deborah were all standing up, looking out into the sea. I did not know if they knew the battle in which I was enmeshed, or if they were simply admiring the beauty of the aqua blue and turquoise Caribbean Sea. It was good to see that they were no longer the size of a Lego figurine, which meant that I was getting closer to that precious sandy shore.

There was no time for sightseeing. I was close, but still too far away. I put my head back into the water and resumed swimming, for my journey was not over. My entire body was fatigued, and I was unable to keep the perfect swimming form I was taught. My fingers became uncupped and spread like I was palming a basketball. I could not complete full strokes with my arms. It was more like slapping at the water instead of full deliberate strokes piercing the water.

Exhaustion kept me from kicking with my hips. I was kicking from my knees, and it was getting me nowhere. I was losing ground and being drawn back into the blue abyss until the cavalry arrived in the form of a third wave. (Divine Completeness and Perfection.)

The wave engulfed me and launched me like a missile with a velocity of 250 meters per second. If the situation wasn't so dangerous and my life didn't depend on it, it would have been fun riding the waves like we did as children at the Jersey shore. I was traveling on course when my left knee and then my right knee hit something. It was the continental shelf, the ocean floor. This was a sign that I was close to the shoreline. The wave dragged me along until it deposited me in water that was shallow enough for me to rest on my hands and knees.

The sea seemed to have a split personality. On the one hand, it gently nudged me forward, still helping me to reach the shore. On the other hand, it reminded me of its power when the undertow tried to pull me back, drawing the sand from under my hands and knees and causing me to sink.

I mustered up enough strength to stand. The sand was still being drawn from beneath my feet, but I was out of the clutches of the riptide and able to move under my own power. I wish I could say that I looked macho like Daniel Craig walking out of the sea in *Casino Royale,* but I looked more like Jonah after being vomited out of the big fish (Jonah 2:10).

The women in our team met me at the water's edge as I exited the water. They surrounded me, Patricia on my right, Deborah on my left, Valerie in front of me, and Kathy behind me. Patricia took my right arm and Deborah took my left. They bombarded me with questions as they led me to the area where they were sitting. Before I could answer one question, I was hit with another. *Are you okay? Are you all right? What happened? Do you want to sit here? How are you feeling?*

When we got to the area, I swung around and collapsed on my back. My energy was spent from my ordeal. Patricia, who was a registered nurse, asked me more specific medical questions while she took my pulse and checked me physically.

"I'm fine. I'm fine," I said. "I just need to catch my breath."

Valerie said, "Brother Rob, we could see that you were in trouble, so we started to pray for you and

Brother Richard." *"Richard?"*

I sat up and said, "Where is Richard?"

We all turned and looked back at the sea, and there was Richard slowly walking out of the water with the aid of the three Haitian boys. There is the number three again. (Divine Completeness and Perfection.) Richard told the boys, *"Mèsi"* (French Creole for "thank you"), and they responded, *"merite"* (French Creole for "you're welcome") as they went running off.

Richard flopped down next to me and let out a big sigh of relief. I asked him if he was all right. He told me that he had a challenging time getting back to shore. He went on to say that when he saw that I was having difficulty making it to shore, he decided to head in himself but kept being pulled back out to sea by the riptide.

His struggle with the water exhausted his strength just as it did with Danny and me. So, he called for the three young Haitian boys and told them to stay around him as he tried to swim to the shoreline . . . and if he sank to rescue him.

The boys told him that they knew a better way to swim back to the shore. They knew how to navigate the sea currents. Instead of swimming straight to shore against the strong riptide, they zig zag their way in, following the currents.

There was not a local YMCA in the village, so they did not have the benefit of being instructed in "proper swimming technique." Instead, they swam on their sides. This was to their advantage in swimming with the currents because all the proper technique I used barely helped me. So, Richard, with the young men surrounding him, followed them as they zigged and zagged their way until Richard was able to stand and walk ashore.

Thank the Most High for His Grace.

Again, the number three played a significant role in these stories. Danny was assisted by three waves. I was aided by three waves. Three young Haitian boys helped Richard. This is a type of the Triune God coming to the rescue of His children.

"For there are three that bear record in heaven, the Father, the Word, and the Holy Ghost: and these three are one" (1 John 5:7).

The point is, whatever you are going through as a child of the Most High, the entire God Head will get involved and bring you out. The Father can and will use anything to deliver His children.

- For Balaam, He used a donkey that saved his life (Numbers 22:23).

- For Elijah, He used Ravens to feed him by the brook Cherith (1 Kings17:6).

- For the Children of Israel, He divided the sea (Exodus 14:21).

- For Daniel, He shut the lion's mouths (Daniel 22:6).

- For the two Hebrew spies, He used Rahab, a prostitute (Joshua 6:25).

- For the three Hebrew boys, He took the heat out of the flames (Daniel 3:25).

- For Joshua, He made the sun stand still (Joshua 10:13).
- For Lazarus, He brought him back to life (John 11:43).
- For Danny and me, He used three waves to save us from drowning.
- Richard, He used three Haitian boys to save him from drowning.

For you, the LORD will bring about deliverance by any means necessary.

You may need a wave of finances.

You may need a wave of healing.

You may need a wave of deliverance.

You may need a wave of salvation.

You may need a wave of provision.

Whatever you need, *"my God shall supply all your need according to His riches in glory by Christ Jesus"* (Philippians 4:19).

God will send three waves in the name of the Father, the Son, and the Holy Spirit.

Just cry out to Him, *"Yo God! Can You Hook Me Up With a Wave?!"*

1. Ed F. Vallowe, *Biblical Mathematics: Keys to Scripture Numerics* (Lexington, SC: Midnight Call, 1995), Pages 53, 55

The "A-Team" making a pit stop
while traveling to the village of Balix.
L–R: Deborah, Valerie, Patricia, Kathy (kneeling), Pastor Carlo
(our Haitian host pastor and founder of New World Missions
for Christ) and Richard Grubb (the mission leader).

This is Robert, our Haitian interpreter. RIP, my brother.

The "A-Team" on the first day in the village of Balix.
L–R: Rob, Kathy, Deborah, Valerie, and Patricia.

The "A-Team": Valerie, Kathy, Patricia, Deborah, and Rob
meeting some of the villagers of Balix.

Deborah (playing the tambourine) and Kathy dancing with Haitian children during children ministry.

Kathy, Patricia, and Deborah dancing with Haitian children during children ministry. Pastor Carlo is in the background, enjoying the time of praise.

*L-R: Patricia, Valerie, Phoebe (The housekeeper),
Kathy, Deborah, and Rob (kneeling). The church/clinic/school
is in the background.*

*Kneeling: Patricia, Valerie, Kathy, Deborah.
Standing: Rob, deacons, and ministers from the
New World Missions for Christ Church. The
church/clinic/school is in the background.*

*Deborah, Kathy, and Patricia sunbathing
after a grueling day at the clinic.*

*Villagers watching the crazy Americans sunbathe.
Deborah and Kathy sunbathing.
Rob in the background, on the left.*

Valerie soaking in the sun while Patricia goes for a dip.

Villagers came to see the crazy Americans sunbathe and swim.

The three Haitian boys.

I just love this picture of this little Haitian girl.
I often wonder how she is doing.

Prayer is our invitation to God to intervene in the affairs of earth. It is our request for Him to work His ways in this world.

—MYLES MUNROE

CHAPTER FOUR

PRAYER CHANGES THINGS

In his book called *The Rewards of Prayer*, R.A. Torrey writes on page 54, *"The one who wishes to succeed in the Christian life must lead a life of prayer. Much of the failure in Christian living today, and Christian work, results from the neglect of prayer.* He goes on to add *"The apostle James told believers in his day that the secret behind the poverty and powerlessness of their lives and service was neglect of prayer.*[2]

Prayer is not a bunch of eloquent words or long-drawn-out Old English phrases. It is an issue of the heart and should be a sincere conversation between you and God. He hears, understands and speaks every language of the world, including that that cannot be uttered, The Living Bible expresses it this way, *"But if we must keep trusting God for something that hasn't happened yet, it teaches us to wait patiently and confidently. And in the same way-by our faith-the Holy Spirit helps us with our daily problems and in our praying. For we don't even know what we should pray for, nor how to pray as we should; but the Holy Spirit prays for us with such feeling that it cannot be expressed in words. And the Father who knows all hearts knows, of course, what the Spirit is saying as he pleads for us in harmony with God's own will.* (Romans 8:25, 26, 27) So, you see, all you have to do is talk to Him. He already knows what it is that you stand in need of. Yet still He is waiting to hear from you.

While growing up, I observed my mother Pearly Mae Robinson, seeking the face of God on her knees in prayer consistently. As I progressed in my adult years, mom never changed the habit of continual prayer whether she was standing or sitting throughout the day.

My dad, on the other hand, was an entirely different story. He was a masterful pianist and played in many churches. However, he fell horribly short as an example of what true godly character should resemble. He abandoned our family when I was about six years old to pursue an alternative lifestyle. He practiced that lifestyle long before marrying my mother. It was a shock to the family!

My mother became an instant single parent. As Mark 4:22 reminds us, *"For there is nothing hid, which shall not be manifested; neither was anything kept secret, but that it should come abroad.* (come to light)"

The last time I saw my father, Horace Robinson alive, was in 1988. He was a walking skeleton. The AIDS virus had ravaged his body. The alternative lifestyle that he so desired and that he abandoned his family for ultimately killed him. He died in January of 1990.

When he left us in1966, my mother was making $85 every two weeks from her job, and the mortgage on our home was $80 a month. During those tough times, I watched the LORD answer her prayers day after day, month after month and year after year. Everything we needed He supplied, whether it was a meal, a bill, home repairs or clothing for our backs, God supplied an answer.

Mom taught me to pray at an early age. She first taught me the familiar children's prayer from the eighteenth century: "Now I lay me down to sleep, I pray the Lord my soul to keep. If I should die before I wake, I pray the Lord my soul to take."

As I got older, she instructed me to talk to our Heavenly Father from my heart. As I grew in the familiarity of the Word of God, I learned the art of prayer, the keys of faith, and the power of confession; this knowledge would eventually serve a great purpose in our destiny. Some years later, my mother would find herself drowning in deep waters of financial crisis and would need God to hook her up too with a wave.

It was February of 2012, I received a call from my cousin Yvonne telling me that my mother's house was on fire. I immediately thought to myself, "Lord what has just happened?" I then grabbed my coat and keys, left work in haste to see what damage had befallen mom's house. Moving at the speed of lightening, I had to park a block away, because of all the police and fire department activity.

As I walked toward the house I was met by a familiar police officer. I told him that it was my mother's house that was on fire. While we were talking, I saw three firemen break in the front door. Without warning, an inferno shot out like fury, scorching the plaster and reaching up to the second-floor window located right above the front door. If that is what the Lake of Fire is like, then I am definitely not going!

I saw my cousin George, who was in the house at the time of the fire, standing a few properties away from the house. I went over and asked him what happened. He said he was upstairs lying down for a nap, when he heard the smoke detector go off. He smelled something burning and thought our younger cousin left a pot burning on the stove. He got up to see, and when George got to the bottom of the steps, he saw the couch across the room completely ablaze. Flames were rapidly engulfing the paneling and setting the ceiling on fire. The couch sat against the wall next to the front door and the hall leading to the kitchen. George said, he ran past the couch to the front door and out of the house just in time before the room became fully engulfed in flames.

I saw my mother walking down the street from the opposite side. She got the news from Yvonne about the fire and left work only to find the house she had grown up in since 1932, ablaze. I walked up and held my mom gently in my arms, just as she had done for me my entire life during times of adversity.

Mom kept her composure, as we watched the flames and smoke pour out of the place she called home since childhood. She was able to maintain such a calm detached demeanor, until the fire was brought under control and a fireman came to speak to us. He walked over and said, "Mrs. Robinson, I am sorry to say that your cat did not make it. We found your cat on the steps. Apparently, it died of smoke inhalation."

That's when Pearly Mae lost it and burst into tears. "I forgot about the cat!" she said. "I forgot about the cat!" I held her as tightly as I could until she completely calmed down.

This was actually the second time the house had been affected by fire. The first incident happened one night in 1934 while my grandparents Leo Sr., Janie Equllar, my mother, her sister, cousin, grandmother and her two brothers were asleep.

The fire started in the Meads' house next door. Regrettably, black smoke penetrated the walls of my mother's home, filling the entire house thereby, causing everyone to fall into a deep sleep. In 1934, there were no smoke detectors like there are today to warn everyone of a fire. Instead, they had the next best thing—a cat named Betsey.

The night of the fire, Betsey went to my grandparent's room and woke my grandmother Janie Equllar out of her sleep first. Mother Janie, then woke my grandfather Leo Sr., aunt Madeline (My mother's sister), and my cousin Mary (My mother's first cousin), who were all sleeping in the same bedroom. Betsey then went to the front bedroom where my mother, Pearly Mae, was sleeping with my great-grandmother Maggie (My grandfather's mother) and woke them.

Betsey then ran to the back bedroom and woke up my two uncles, Leo Jr. and Albert (My mother's two brothers). My family was able to get out of the house and not fall victim to deadly smoke inhalation because of Betsey the cat! *Yo God what a Wave!*

To their surprise and dismay, when they exited the house, all the neighbors of the block were standing in the street. No one banged on the door, yelled, or screamed to warn them there was a fire. If it was not for Betsey the cat, my grandparents, great-grandmother, uncles, aunt, cousin, and mother would have died that night in 1934, and I would not be here today to tell the story, and you would not be reading "Yo God! Can You Hook Me Up With a Wave?!" at this very moment! The Lord can and will use anyone and anything to save your life especially when your life is connected to saving others. For after this fire, a total of 30 children consisting of, grandchildren and great-grandchildren were born out of our family legacy, from those whom Betsey saved out of the fire on that day.

Let's get back to February 2012. At the time of this second fire, my mother was eighty-three years old. (Let me just say, that my mom is still vibrant as ever and employed with the Montgomery County Courthouse at 90 years of age). As her only child, I took control of the situation and interacted with the police, fire department, Red Cross, and the newspaper. Also, due to the fire, I without question became involved in my mother's finances after discovering that she re-mortgaged and owed $96,000.00 on a thirty-year mortgage on this same house. Her monthly payment was $850 a month at an 8.5 percent interest rate. She had been hoodwinked and bamboozled by a predatory lender.

I said, "Mom, you would have to live until you are 113 years of age to pay this mortgage off!"

What angered me the most, was that she was in debt because she was trying to take care of our relatives. I asked my mother to let me help her get out of this debt. She agreed and gave me power of attorney, enabling me to manage her finances.

Galatians 6:7 tells us, *"for whatsoever a man soweth, that shall he also reap."* Or, as it is usually quoted, "you reap what you sow."

My mother is a giver. She has sown a lot of kindness and has helped a multitude of people in the community. As the news quickly spread through the towns "grapevine" of the tragedy of the fire at my mother's home, people began giving money in support of her. I managed the funds, prayed for supernatural debt cancellation, received funds and initiated *"project get-out-of-debt."*

Slowly but surely, I was able to pay off my mother's debt, one bill at a time. I was surprised however, to discover how some creditors made paying off the debt so difficult to accomplish.

For example, Mom had taken out a line of credit for $7,000 at 18 percent interest and then used that money to pay other loans and bills. Later, I went to the company and spoke with the manager, telling him that I was there to pay off my mother's loan. I showed him the power of attorney, but he said that I could not pay off the debt. He told me that it was because he could not give out personal information of other clients.

I said, "I don't want any personal information. Here is her account number. I'm just here to pay off Pearly Mae's loan."

He still refused to allow me to pay it off.

We eventually got into a heated argument about creditors, money owed, predatory lending, and obligation. He said that my mother would have to come to the office and pay it off herself. I looked him straight in his eyes and told him I would be right back.

I walked to my car and called my mother and told her what had just transpired. I told her that I was going to the bank to get a cashier's check for the amount of the loan and would be by to pick her up.

Within an hour, we were back at the loan company. I asked for the manager by name. The employee that I spoke with said that he was unavailable. I could see him sitting in his office. He just refused to come out and speak with us because he knew that we meant business and that my mother was about to be set free from the bondage of his chokehold of debt. No longer would she be a prisoner of indebtedness to his company's 18 percent interest.

I strongly affirmed our reason for returning loudly enough for the manager to hear me. We sat at the desk while the employee pulled the loan information up on the computer. It was a "praise the Lord" moment when I handed the check over to the employee, which completely satisfied the financial obligation of the original $7000.00 debt and pried the creditor's claws from around my mother's neck. PRAYER, PRAYER, PRAYER, *Another wave of a Miracle!*

2. R.A. Torrey, *The Rewards of Prayer,* (New Kensington, PA: Whitaker House, 2012), Page 54

The true means of a man is not how he behaves in moments of comfort and convenience, but how he stands at times of controversy and challenges.

—MARTIN LUTHER KING JR.

CHAPTER FIVE

SOMETHING GOOD CAN COME OUT OF THE FIRE

There was much cleaning to do after the fire. You never know how much is lost until the flames have been extinguished. I gathered as many memories as I could that were not totally destroyed. There was still an old cable bill that had yet to be paid. Mom owed close to $500 on her bill. The bill was so high because of relatives living in the house ordering all sorts of different channels. The money was now due.

When I entered the cable company's office, there was no one there but me and the two employees working behind the counter. I walked up to one of the young ladies. She did not even raise her head to acknowledge my presence. She kept looking down and told me to stand behind the line. There was a roped-off area for people to stand. I turned and looked at the area, then turned back around and told her there was nobody in the store but me. She said, "You still have to stand behind the line and wait to be called."

I was a little annoyed at her nonchalant attitude and poor customer service, but I walked and stood behind the line, trying not to get angrier. As I stood there waiting to be called, I saw my reflection in the window. I really looked a hot mess.

I had been crawling around in the burned-out house all morning salvaging anything I could. My mother kept sending me in the house to look for this and to see if I could find that. I was covered in soot and grime from head to toe. The stench of smoke followed me like the smell of a skunk. I looked impoverished, but this should not have been a reason for the unsatisfactory customer service.

The young lady finally called me to come to the counter. (Remember, I did what I was told and stood behind the line and waited patiently to be called.) However, her attitude never changed.

I told her that my mother's house caught on fire and I was here to pay off the cable bill and to close the account. She said, with a bad attitude, "We cannot close the account without the equipment."

I said, "You don't understand, the house burned up. The equipment that was in the house is either burned up or damaged."

She said, very sarcastically, "You have to bring in the equipment in order for me to close the account."

I told her like Arnold Schwarzenegger told the police officer in the movie *Terminator*, "I'll be back!"

I drove back to the house, grabbed a green

thirty-pound trash bag, and went from room to room gathering cable receivers and remotes, putting them in the bag. The cable equipment was either water damaged, burned up, smoke damaged, or all three. But the cable company employee said I had to bring in the equipment to cancel the account, so that's exactly what she was going to get!

Within an hour, I was back in the store, standing behind the line waiting. And once again I was the only customer in the store. The other young lady said to me, very pleasantly, "Can I help you?" I pointed to her coworker and said, "No, thank you. I'm waiting for her."

The employee, with whom I'd spoken to the first time, looked at me over top of her glasses and proceeded to look down at her counter as she continued doing whatever it was she was doing. Five minutes or more went by and she finally looked at me and said, very unpleasantly, "Can I help you?" I said yes and walked up to the counter, telling her again that I wished to cancel my mother's account. She said, "You have to turn in the equipment before the account can be canceled."

"No problem," I said. I bent down, picked up the heavy, smelly, dirty trash bag, and placed it on her counter. She leaned back quickly and said, "What is this?"

I said, "You wanted the equipment . . . well . . . here it is!"

She struggled to pick up the hefty bag and immediately placed it on the floor. As she opened it up, the stench from the burned-up equipment caused her to throw her head back and speedily shut the bag.

She turned to me and said, "What am I supposed to do with this?"

I said, "You wanted the equipment, so here it is.

Now cancel my mother's account!" Her co-worker was hysterical.

By the grace of God, I was able to pay off all of my mother's bills except the mortgage. What a fight I had with them. Let's just say that it was quite an ordeal. Mom needed a tidal wave of a miracle to defeat that mortgage demon. However, God was already working in the background, orchestrating a victorious outcome to fulfill His divine will.

The mortgage company and I were locked into a fifteen-round heavyweight fight reminiscent of the Muhammad Ali and Joe Frazier "Thrilla in Manila." I asked them why they would agree to grant a $96,000 thirty-year mortgage to an eighty-three-year-old woman. It would be totally impossible for such an elderly individual to pay back a thirty-year note. The person would have had to live to be 113 years old to fulfil paying off that debt.

They still demanded their money regardless.

I then asked why they approved a $96,000 mortgage on a house that was valued at $40,000 to $45,000 maximum; they had no answer. This back and forth went on for about a year. But prayer for a supernatural debt cancellation miracle was still going on. I reached a point where I was fed up and I did not want to fight and argue anymore. It was obvious to me that

my mother fell victim to the predatory lending prac-
tices of a crooked, greedy, lender. I finally told them,
"You should have never lent the money to my mother.
If you want the house, come and get it."

Hence, the warfare began. During that year of
engaging in battle with the mortgage company, we
prayed and repeatedly confessed supernatural debt
cancellation over moms' finances. Our family believed
by faith, that the LORD would answer our prayers. As
a family, we waged war together in seeking the face of
God continually through prayer.

Miraculously, as an answer to prayer, months later
my mother received a letter from the predatory lender,
while temporarily living with me. The contents of the
letter informed her that the house was no longer val-
ued at $96,000. In addition, the house would be writ-
ten off without any lawsuits pursuant to the matter.
Further, the title deed to the property would be sent
within five business days. Immediately, mom asked
me for clarity. I said, "I believe it means that you just
received supernatural debt cancellation on a $96,000
mortgage." I told her that I would seek legal counsel to
verify the authenticity of the letter and that is exactly
what I did.

Later, while meeting with my attorney, after hand-
ing him the letter, he began reading while gently sitting back in his chair. A few seconds elapsed, and he
lowered it enough to give a brief glimpse at me over
the top of the document, in a continual motion he
raised it ever so slightly and continued to read.

In astonishment, he handed the letter back to me

while confirming its authenticity and said, "I must say, in all the years I have been practicing real estate law, this is the first time I have heard of a mortgage being forgiven." He was right, neither had any of us experienced the hand of God from a spiritually creative stand point do such a thing. Isaiah 64:4 proclaims, *"For since the beginning of the world men have not heard, nor perceived by the ear, neither hath the eye seen, O God, beside thee, what he hath prepared for him that waiteth for him."*

This gave me an opportunity to witness to him, of the goodness of the Most High God, while inquiring about the title to the property. He assured me that it was free and clear, and my mom could do whatever she wanted to do with it. Without a doubt, we decided to sell the property. We sold it, just as it was burned up and all.

It was the first time prior to marrying my dad, that mom was completely out of debt. Not only did he make her a single parent in an instant, but my father had also left her with a mountain of debt. But GOD! Now my mother didn't owe anything to anyone. No more harassing phone calls from debt collectors, no more letters from bill collectors, no more robbing Peter to pay Paul. She was financially free.

My mother is a very proud woman. She does not wear her emotions on her sleeve. Maybe it's because she had to work so hard, alone while providing for her family. She looked at me in that moment, with great astonishment of the miraculous power of God, with tears of joy swelling in her eyes and said, "Yes, I am out of debt."

What a WAVE!, a big, supernatural, financial wave that washed away all her debt. The song says, *"Jesus paid it all, all to Him I owe, sin hath left a crimson stain but he washed it white as snow"*. I believe that the Father does not want any of His children drowning in a sea of debt. The bible says that *"But my God would supply all of your need according to His riches in glory by Christ Jesus"* (Phil 4:19). I believe that He can send you a wave and do the same for you as he did for my mother. No gimmicks; no $1,000, $500, $100 church offering lines—just pure faith, trust, and belief in the Word of God.

Surely, we need wisdom in escaping the trappings of this Babylonian financial system. James 1:5 says, *"If any of you lack wisdom, let him ask of God, that giveth to all men liberally, and upbraideth not; and it shall be given him."* **Be led by The Holy Spirit in all financial transactions.**

Just cry out to Him and say, Like Danny *"Yo God! Can you Hook Me Up With a Wave?!"*

Don't give up. Don't lose hope. Don't sell out.

—CHRISTOPHER REEVE

CHAPTER SIX

DESPERATE TIMES DEMAND DESPERATE MEASURES

Danny was in a desperate situation fighting against the oceans riptide. No one could help him but God. So, he cried out to the Lord with a loud voice for help.

Are you in need of help right now? Desperate times demand desperate actions. You too need to cry out to the Most High for help. Are there people who are hindering you? Maybe someone biologically or spiritually who laments your success. Whoever it is, don't allow them to hinder you from receiving all that the Lord has promised to you in His word. The words for you today are Desperation and Perseverance, by laying hold of the promises (2 Pet 1:4). They are yours, by faith. Meditate on these promises and watch God send a wave of revival in your spirit.

Right now, I want to go to the Word of God and take a few moments to encourage you, by observing how a gentleman's desperate attempt to get to Christ, was rewarded by a supernatural miracle from the hand of the Master Himself. Blind Bartimaeus understood the saying "Desperate times demands desperate measures."

Listen to Mark 10:46, *"And they came to Jericho: and as He went out of Jericho with His disciples and a great number of people, blind Bartimaeus, the son of Timaeus, sat by the highway side begging. And when he heard that it was Jesus of Nazareth, he began to cry out, and say, Jesus, thou son of David, have mercy on me. And many charged him that he should hold his peace: but he cried the more a great deal, Thou son of David, have mercy on me."*

Blind Bartimaeus was considered a nobody. There are many people around the world because of disabilities, who are considered insignificant because they lack the ability to help themselves. You may be treading the waters of sickness, poverty, financial ruin or, emotional disaster, barely surviving, but you are precious to the Savior. Christ will travel through the broken roads of your life and restore you too, if you will take a moment to ask.

The people from whom Bartimaeus sought help would not or could not give him what he really needed. Nobody but Christ had the power to heal his blindness on that day. It is a good idea to be very particular about who you ask for help. Be mindful of where your help comes from. Let's look at Luke's version of the story found in Luke 18:35–36.

"And it came to pass, that as He was come nigh unto

Jericho a certain blind man sat by the wayside 'begging: and hearing the multitude pass by, he asked what it meant."

It was not a customary practice for Hebrews to travel through Jericho to get to Jerusalem. However, The Savior made a special trip through Jericho because He knew that there was someone He needed to see; someone who could not physically see him, blind Bartimaeus.

Robbers and thieves often terrorized those traveling the road from Jericho to Jerusalem. In fact, this is the same road where the story of the Good Samaritan took place (Luke 10:30–37).

If you will take a moment to ask. With all the churches in the area where you live, there should be a buzz about The Savior of the World. Churches should be making life changing, eternal differences, by the power of the Holy Spirit in the lives of believers because The Savior is still passing by!

According to verse 37, *"And they told him, that Jesus of Nazareth was passing by."* The people told Bartimaeus that Jesus of Nazareth was passing by:

- The Holy One, who fed five thousand and then four thousand people
- The Holy One, who healed a deaf and dumb man
- The Holy One, who stilled the raging sea
- The Holy One, who healed Jairus's daughter
- The Holy One, who healed the woman with the issue of blood

- The Holy One, who delivered a demon-possessed man

- The Holy One, who commands demons to flee

There is a song that has been sung in many churches down through the years, the words and music written by Bill Harman (Copyright 1958 and renewed in 1986 by Gospel Publishing House) that goes like this; *"Reach out and touch the Lord as He goes by. You will find He's not too busy to hear your hearts cry. He is passing by this moment your need to supply. Reach out and touch the Lord as He goes by."* It is the responsibility of every born-again believer to tell the world about the Risen Savior.

I'm here to tell you that the Savior is passing by right now.

- He can and is willing to heal you.

- He can and is willing to save you.

- He can and is willing to deliver you.

- He can and is willing to provide for you.

Look at Bartimaeus' response after he heard it was Christ. Mark 10:47 reads, *"And when he heard that it was Jesus of Nazareth, he began to cry out, and say, Jesus, Thou Son of David, have mercy on me!"*

By calling Him the Son of David, Bartimaeus acknowledged several key points:

- He was the promised Messiah.

- He was the answer he needed.

- The Son of God had the power to create a miracle.

- Bartimaeus was crying out in faith to the True Deliverer for deliverance.

The religious folks tried to shut him up. Indeed, Mark 10:48 tells us, *"And many charged him that he should hold his peace: but he cried the more a great deal, Thou Son of David, have mercy on me."*

Even today, some religious folks would tell you it doesn't take all that. Sometimes it takes all that and then some.

Blind Bartimaeus was in a desperate situation just like Danny, who was being slowly pulled out to sea by the rip current. Bartimaeus did not care who was around, who heard him, or what they said or thought. Instead, *"he cried out all the more, 'Son of David, have mercy on me!'"*

When people know without a doubt that they need a miracle, they do not care who's around or who hears them. People yell for less important issues such as their favorite football teams during record breaking temperatures in the dead of winter. They yell for their favorite political candidate at rallies. They march in parades hollering their sexual preferences. If they can yell during these occasions, then surely, we can yell for Christ the Savior to save us in our trouble.

Don't let people shut you up until you get what you want from GOD. Don't let anything or anyone get in your way. Tell them if they can't help you, then please don't block you . . .move out of your way and don't try to stop you. I want to tell you that all of those around Bartimaeus were seeing people. What do I mean? They all had the ability to see, none of them were blind, yet none of them could see the power that the Holy One of Israel possessed to change their lives at that moment. Only Bartimaeus yelled desperately for help while The Savior was passing in the crowd. Although he was blind, he could see with faith on the inside that eternal help was right within his reach. He had only one moment of opportunity to receive his miracle.

Unknown to Bartimaeus that was going to be Christ's last time passing that way. He was on His way to Jerusalem, to Golgotha (Hebrew: The place of a skull) to be crucified for the sins of the world. If he would have listened to the naysayers, Bartimaeus would have missed his greatest opportunity and we would have lost one of the most powerful miracles of healing documented in the Word of God.

The bible says in verse 49 of Mark 10, *"And Jesus stood still, and commanded him to be called."* The Master stood still, the God of all comfort stood still. Bartimaeus had a one on one audience with the Son of the Living God, the Savior of the World. My LORD *"stood still"* and took the time to minister to a poor soul in a deplorable condition. Such grace! How many people do we pass going and coming from church functions who need ministry? Yet Christ heard a cry of hope and desperation and stopped to see about a nobody. We can never be too busy to minister to people in grievous situations, as the Holy Spirit leads.

To you who are reading this book, I'm telling you

that the Most High has heard your cry. Be of good cheer, take courage, and be of good comfort. (Joshua 1:9) Rise, He is calling you. *"Draw nigh to God, and He will draw nigh to you"* (James 4:8a).

In biblical times, and in parts of the world still today, people had to wear clothes that depicted their station or status in life. It was and is a caste system.

Bartimaeus wore beggar's clothes. The garments identified him as a beggar, a downtrodden outcast and vagabond.

But verse 50 says, *"And he, casting away his garment, rose, and came to Jesus."*

Bartimaeus heard the call of The Son of God and responded. He threw off those things that identified him as a beggar, a vagabond, an outcast, a part of the downtrodden, and he came to Christ. By faith, you can throw aside those things that have you bound.

- Throw off your doubt.

- Throw off your fears.

- Throw off your pride.

- Throw off confusion.

- Throw off low self-esteem.

- Throw off insecurities.

- Throw off unbelief.

- Throw off failure

According to verse 51, *"And Jesus answered and said unto him, what wilt thou that I should do unto thee?"*

He knew what Bartimaeus wanted, but He asked anyway.

In verse 51, Bartimaeus replies.

"Lord, that I might receive my sight."

Bartimaeus had to open his mouth and declare and agree with the Word (John 1:1). The Most High wants you to be specific when you pray. Bartimaeus was very specific *". . . Lord, that I might receive my sight."*

What do you want the Lord to do for you? He wants you to be specific.

People ask for prayer in a general way. They say please pray for my family. Pray what about your family—healing, salvation, provision? What?

Philippians 4:6 says, *"Be careful [anxious] for nothing; but in everything by prayer and supplication, with thanksgiving let your requests be made known to God".*

As the Scripture says, let your requests be made known . . . be specific when you pray.

Mark 10, verse 52 says, *"And Jesus said unto him, go thy way; thy faith hath made thee whole. And immediately he received his sight and followed Jesus in the way."*

According to Luke 18:43, *"And immediately he received his sight, and followed Him, glorifying God: and all the people, when they saw it, gave praise to God."*

Remember that there were people who tried to shut him up. After Bartimaeus' interaction with Christ, all the people gave praise to God—I call them bandwagon praisers.

People in your life will try to keep you from getting blessed, and when you do get blessed they will want to join in on the praising. The Enemy (the devil) is always trying to keep people from praising and crying out to the Lord. Do not let anyone or anything keep you from getting all that the LORD has for you and your family. He is just a pray away.

If you are in an impossible situation like Blind Bartimaeus, Danny or my Mom, even if you are in a not so desperate situation, but it is still a situation that calls for outside help, cry out to Elohim like Danny and say, *"Yo God! Can You Hook Me Up With a Wave?!"*

We make choices every day that can and will affect our lives and the lives of our loved ones positively or negatively.

—Rob Robinson

CHAPTER SEVEN

OBEY THE VOICE OF THE LORD

In his book entitled *The Voice of a Prophet*, A.W. Tozer, writes on page 71, *"God wants to create a divine awareness in us so that we can see and hear the voice of God. In order for that to happen, we must be detached from all outside interference".*[3] We must be careful not to allow other voices to bombard our spiritual ears when given divine direction from the Holy Spirit. Case in point, in 2006, I was the president of a 501(c)(3) organization founded by my family called "People Helping People, Families Helping Families." The organization received gently used furniture, clothing, household goods and gave them to needy families and individuals. We received so many donations, that we needed a warehouse or some type of building to store the items.

I found a five-bedroom, one-bath home with a detached garage property. It was definitely a "fixer upper." The woman who had lived there passed away.

She was a tremendous hoarder. Trash and junk littered the property from one end to the other. You had to follow a path to walk through the kitchen, dining room, living room, and to the stairs.

As part of the purchase agreement, the family cleaned out all the trash, but the place was still a dump. My wife Monica said to me, "Are you sure about this?" She was getting what is called "a check in her spirit" not to purchase the property.

I confidently said, "Yes, I'm sure. We can fix the house up, rent it out, and use the garage for storage for our non-profit organization."

She said, "All right, if you think so."

It sounded like a plan—a plan made of Swiss cheese, full of holes.

I sat at the settlement table for the closing across from the two sellers, their real estate agent, the owner and a staff member of the Abstract Company where the closing was being held. We went over the paperwork and it was now time to sign the papers. I was handed a pen, and I heard a soft voice say, *"Don't do it."*

I shrugged it off, bent down to write, and heard it again. "Don't do it."

I sat back, and the seller's real estate agent asked me if everything was all right.

I will not get into a theological debate whether the God still speaks to His people today. I know my Evangelical Fundamentalist brothers and sisters (and I do call them my brothers and sisters of the faith) teach that the Most High does not speak to His people anymore. He speaks through His Word, they say, and they point to Scriptures like Hebrews 1:1–2, which says, *"God, who at Sundry (various) times and in divers manner spake in time past unto the fathers by the prophets, hath in these last days spoken unto us by His Son, whom He hath appointed heir of all things, by whom also He made the worlds;"* and 1 Corinthians 13:8–10, which teaches, *"Charity (Love) never faileth: but whether there be prophecies, they shall fail; whether there be tongues, they shall cease; whether there is knowledge, it shall vanish away. For we know in part, and we prophesy in part. But when that which is perfect has come, then that which is in part shall be done away."*

Evangelicals teach that when Sha'ul (Paul) wrote *"when that which is perfect is come,"* he is referring to when the Bible is complete. Now that we have the completed Cannon of Scripture, there is no need for Scripture Gifts or for the Most High to speak directly to people.

On the other hand, my Pentecostal, Charismatic, and Word of Faith brothers and sisters believe that the Most High still speaks to His people. They believe that the Spiritual Gifts are still in operation today. They quote verses such as Joel 2:28–29, which states, *"And it shall come to pass afterward, that I will pour out My Spirit on all flesh; your sons and your daughters shall prophesy, your old men shall dream dreams, your young men shall see visions: and also, upon the servants and upon the handmaids in those days will I pour out My Spirit."*

They will get no argument from me. I believe that when I heard, *"Don't do it,"* it was a warning from the

Most High that I was about to enter into a contract that would bring suffering to my family. Why wouldn't our Heavenly Father warn his children that they are heading for trouble? He is the only Omniscient and Omnipresent God! He can use any means necessary to warn and protect His people from hurt, harm, or danger. After hearing the warning, I paused because I knew it was the Holy Spirit. The owner of the Abstract Company asked if I was all right. He had no idea of the battle raging inside of me. I looked at the five faces watching, all of whom did not resemble me, and pride rose to the occasion. My thoughts turned from reversing the curse of poverty to the transference of wealth to my family. Nevertheless, I heard another voice, the voice of pride in my head said everyone is looking at you. You can't get up and leave now. What are they going to say about you wasting everybody's time?

Old man pride caused me to quench the Spirit and sign the papers. I should have listened to the voice of God and taken direction from Proverbs 16:18, *"Pride goeth before destruction, and a haughty spirit before a fall."*

The purchase was a wrong decision. I bought an investment property that I thought I could eventually flip, but instead *I* got flipped. I guess I watched too many house-flipping shows on television.

It took hard work, but I was able to get the property up to code and was granted a U&O (Uses and Occupancy Certificate) from the Code Enforcement Department and rented out the house.

For the first couple of years, things were good. I

had good tenants who paid pretty much on time, but then I had a series of bad renters who didn't pay. After a few years of sewer repairs, a new roof, plumbing problems, a new hot water heater, new windows, new carpeting, painting, drywall repairs, taxes, and unpaid rent, it all started to add up. We were unable to pay on the $118,000 mortgage for two years, plus we owed $11,000 in back taxes. The last tenant destroyed the property. There were bedbugs, roaches, mice, and fleas throughout the property. In the basement, there were dog feces that sent a putrid odor throughout the house. It was in such deplorable condition that upon walking into the garage and exiting into my car, as I looked down at my cache jeans, little black fleas were dancing all around me. I drove straight to Home Depot to purchase several cans of bombs for bug extermination. I called Monica my wife and discussed the situation. Her instructions to me were, don't bring those fleas in my house. I will leave you some extra clothes to change into on the side of the garage when you arrive home. I was not allowed to enter my home or garage but had to change outside. From there I threw the infested clothes into the car and set off the bombs that I'd bought at home depot. All of this because I did not heed the strict command of the Word of the Lord.

As time went on, we received letters and phone calls from the mortgage company along with tax delinquency warnings from the county. There was absolutely nothing I could do. I did not have money to pay the mortgage, the taxes, make repairs or clean the property so that it could be rented again.

I thought back to the moment at settlement when I heard that still small voice said, "Don't do it." This caused me to repent. I cried out to the Father, asking Him to forgive me for not obeying and following the leading of His Spirit. I then repented to my wife for not listening to her as well and for getting us in a serious financial predicament. She also asked me to forgive her, for she felt strongly that we should not have purchased the property, but she did not press the issue.

Once we reconciled with the LORD and with each other, our focus turned to how our Heavenly Father was going to get us out of the financial whirlpool. We needed Him to hook us up with a wave.

Again, Monica and I launched into some serious praying and confessing to the Most High for supernatural debt cancellation. We confessed *"favour with God and man"* (Luke 2:52). We *"called those things which were not, as though they were"* (Romans 4:17). We began speaking that all our bills were paid off and that we were out of debt. We also started confessing and believing the Most High for a 4x4 vehicle without a car note for the winter weather.

To be forgiven of a $118,000 mortgage and be blessed with a 4x4 vehicle without a car note is impossible, right?

Wrong!

"For with God nothing shall be impossible" (Luke 1:37). Because *"the just shall live by faith"* (Romans 1:17).

Along with praying and confessing, we also did

what we needed to do as far as watching how we spent our money and looking for sales, deals, and bargains. We asked for wisdom in all financial decisions.

Months went by, and the threatening calls and the letters from the mortgage company and the county demanding payment continued. Surprisingly, in 2013, we received a letter in the mail from the mortgage company. I did not want to open it. I thought it was another demand letter. The suspense was too much so, I opened it, and *I Got My Wave!!!*

The letter said something like this, "Dear Mr. Robinson, we are no longer pursuing the repayment of your $118,000 mortgage. *"WHAT???"* You are forgiven of the responsibility of this matter. However, you are still responsible for payment of the taxes on the property. In a few weeks, we will mail you the mortgage release and the title to the property."

Praise the name of the LORD Most High!!!

We had supernatural debt cancellation of a $118,000 mortgage. In addition, the mortgage company was sending me the title to the property. This was wave number one. When the title came in the mail in my name, I went straight to the realtor and showed him the debt cancellation letter. His response to me was that in 35 years of selling real estate he had never witnessed a mortgage forgiveness. He made a copy of the letter and shared it with his fellow brokers. Immediately I said, "Put the property up for sale just as it is—fleas, bedbugs, roaches, dog feces—all of it!" A few months went by, and I got a call from my realtor telling me there was an investor who wanted to buy the property. I showed the investor the property myself. A couple of weeks later, we were sitting at the settlement table.

This time, I did not hear, *"Don't do it."*

He bought the investment property—fleas, bed-bugs, roaches, mice, dog feces, and all for $45,000. With the proceeds, I paid the realtor his fee and paid off the $11,000 in back taxes owed to the county. That was the *second wave!*

With the remaining profit from the sale I went to a car dealership. I surprised Monica by purchasing a 4x4 vehicle, fully loaded. That was the third wave of Divine Completeness and Perfection. *"Won't He do it!"*

Whatever situation you find yourself in that seems too impossible for you to get out of, you can call on the Lord for his help. The chorus of one of my favorite hymns growing up goes like this, *"Ask the Savior to help you to comfort strengthen and keep you, He is willing to help you, He will carry you through."* Examine your circumstance. Was the circumstance birthed out of your disobedience? Did you miss or ignore the voice of the Most High? If so, repent. Sincerely ask for forgiveness and fall upon the Father's grace and mercy. *"If we confess our sins, He is faithful and just to forgive us our sins, and to cleanse us from all unrighteousness"* (1 John 1:9).

He is loving, kind and *"willing to help you."*

Take comfort in knowing that if your heart condemns you, God is greater than your heart, grace is always available. *"But unto every one of us is given* grace according to the measure of the gift of Christ." (Ephesians 4:7)

In John 16:33, we learn, *"These things I have spoken to you, that in Me ye may have peace. In the world ye shall have tribulation: but be of good cheer; I have overcome the world."* Psalm 34:6 also tells us, *"This poor man cried out, and the LORD heard him, and saved him out of all his troubles."*

Whatever your plight may be, just look to God the Father and cry out to Him,

"Yo God! Can You Hook Me Up With a Wave?!"

---

3. A. W. Tozer, *Voice of a Prophet* (Bloomington, MN: Bethany House Publishers, 2014), Page 71